Countries of the World

The Netherlands

by Michael Dahl

Content Consultant:
Peter Theunissen
Royal Netherlands Embassy

Bridgestone Books
an Imprint of Capstone Press

Bridgestone Books are published by Capstone Press
1710 Roe Crest Drive, North Mankato, Minnesota 56003
www.capstonepub.com

Library of Congress Cataloging-in-Publication Data
Dahl, Michael S.
    The Netherlands/by Michael Dahl.
    p. cm.—(Countries of the world)
    Includes bibliographical references and index.
    Summary: An introduction to the geography, history, economy, culture, and people of the
Netherlands.
    ISBN-13: 978-1-56065-568-8 (hardcover)   ISBN-10: 1-56065-568-2 (hardcover)
    ISBN-13: 978-0-7368-8379-5 (paperback)   ISBN-10: 0-7368-8379-7 (paperback)
    1. Netherlands—Juvenile literature. [1. Netherlands.] I. Title. II. Series: Countries of the
world (Mankato, Minn.)
DJ18.D27   1998
949.2—dc21   97-5816

Photo Credits
Capstone Press, 5 (top)
Capstone Press Archives, 5 (bottom)
Dutch Tourist Board, 20
Embassy of the Netherlands, 8, 14
International Stock/Chad Ehlers, cover; Ronn Maratea, 16
Root Resources/Larry Schaefer, 6
James Rowan, 10
Unicorn Stock/Andre Jenny, 12; Chuck Schmeiser, 18

Printed in the United States of America in North Mankato, Minnesota.
012012
006536CGVMI

Table of Contents

Fast Facts

Official Name: The Kingdom of the Netherlands
Capital: Amsterdam
Population: More than 15 million
Language: Dutch
Religions: Roman Catholic, Protestant

Size: 16,033 square miles (41,686 square kilometers) *The Netherlands is a little less than twice the size of New Jersey.*
Major Crops: Grains, sugar beets, tulips

Maps

Flag

The Netherlands' flag has three stripes. The top stripe is red. A white stripe is in the middle. The bottom stripe is blue. These three colors are the national colors of the Netherlands.

Currency

The unit of currency in the Netherlands is the euro. The Netherlands is a country in the European Union that uses the euro.

In the early 2000s, 1 U.S. dollar equaled about .90 euro. One Canadian dollar equaled about .65 euro.

The Low Country

The Netherlands is a small, flat country in western Europe. It is between Germany and Belgium. The Netherlands also controls some islands. The islands are faraway in the Caribbean Sea.

The Netherlands has a queen. It also has the States General. The States General is a group of people. They help make laws.

Holland is another name for the Netherlands. People in the Netherlands are called Dutch or Netherlanders.

Long ago, the North Sea covered the country's low ground. The Dutch used windmills to pump water back to the sea. A windmill is a machine moved by the wind. They also built strong walls called dikes to keep the water out. The Dutch still fight to keep their land from flooding. Today, water is pumped out by windmills and powered machines.

Windmills pump water back to the sea.

Going to School

Children in the Netherlands attend public school for free. The government also helps pay for private schools. About 75 percent of children go to private schools. Some private schools are religious. Religious means having to do with God.

Dutch children start primary school at age four or five. This is like elementary school in North America. They stay in primary school until age 12. They learn Dutch, science, math, and history. They also have art and physical education classes.

After primary school, children go to secondary school. This is like high school in North America. Children begin to learn English in secondary school. In the Netherlands, some secondary schools train students for factory work. Other schools are for students who want to go to college.

Children stay in primary school until age 12.

Home and Sports

Dutch houses are known for their special look. Many houses have gables. A gable is part of a roof. Gables can look like bells, steps, or triangles. Buildings are usually made of brick.

Many Dutch people enjoy sports. Thirty percent of Dutch people belong to sports clubs. There are more than 35,000 sports clubs in the Netherlands.

Voetbal (VOOT-bahl) is the national sport of the Netherlands. Voetbal is known as soccer in North America. Tennis is the second most popular sport in the Netherlands. In the winter, ice-skating is a favorite sport.

Fierljeppen (feerl-YEP-pen) is an old Dutch sport. People use a long pole to leap over canals and ditches. Canals are specially built waterways. Some people in the northern part of the Netherlands still play fierljeppen.

Dutch buildings are known for their gables.

Dutch Food

Many Dutch people eat bread for breakfast. They put toppings on the bread. Butter, jelly, meat, and cheese are some favorite toppings.

The Netherlands is famous for its cheese. People make many different kinds. Edam and Gouda cheeses are named after Dutch cities. Cheese is an important part of many Dutch meals.

For lunch, Dutch people usually have bread and toppings. Sometimes they eat a sandwich made with buttered bread and meat. It is called an uitsmijter (OUTS-may-ter). An uitsmijter is usually topped with two fried eggs. Dutch people also eat something warm for lunch such as soup.

For most Dutch people, supper is the main meal. Usually, the meal starts with soup. Meat, fish, and potatoes make up the rest of the meal.

The Dutch enjoy eating seafood. Herring and eel are two popular fish. Many people eat herring raw.

The Netherlands is famous for its cheese.

Cities and Canals

Amsterdam is the capital of the Netherlands. People in this city are known for working with diamonds. People from around the world send diamonds to Amsterdam. Workers cut and polish the diamonds. Polish means to shine.

Rotterdam is the second largest city in the Netherlands. It is also one of the world's busiest ports. Ships travel from Germany to Japan by passing through Rotterdam.

The Netherlands has many canals that cut through cities and the countryside. Canals help drain water from the land. People also use the canals for traveling by boat. In the winter, canals freeze. Skaters race up and down the ice.

The Dutch enjoy growing flowers. Even in cities, there are many gardens. The tulip is the Netherlands' most famous flower. Special tulip days are held in the spring. Dutch tulips are sold all over the world.

The tulip is the Netherlands' most famous flower.

Animals

The Netherlands is home to small animals. Very few large animals live there. This is because the country is small and crowded. More than 15 million people live in the Netherlands. There is not much room for wildlife.

Dutch people built dikes to keep water from flooding land. Sometimes this hurt wildlife. Some animals need watery areas to live. There were none of these places left for animals. Today, Dutch people are trying to help wildlife. They made special water areas for the birds and animals.

Fox and deer live in the northern parts of the Netherlands. Boar also live there. A boar is a wild pig.

Many birds live by the mud that gathers by river mouths. These birds are called wading birds. They have long legs. Long legs help them walk in water. Herons are common wading birds.

Herons are wading birds that live in the mud by rivers.

17

Clothes

Today, many Dutch people dress like most North Americans. In the past, they had special clothes. These clothes are called traditional dress. Each area had its own type of traditional dress.

Men wore black jackets and pants as their special clothes. They also dressed in colorful shirts and hats.

Women dressed in colorful skirts and aprons for their special clothes. They also wore short-sleeved jackets.

Women wore head coverings, too. Some women had hats that covered their ears. Others had pointed hats with curled ends by each ear.

Many Dutch people wore wooden shoes called clogs. Some people still wear clogs.

Today, some people in small villages still wear traditional dress. Others wear these clothes only on holidays.

Some people wear traditional dress on holidays.

Holidays

Winter is a time of holidays in the Netherlands. Dutch people celebrate Christmas. They also have Saint Nicholas Day on December 6. It honors a Catholic saint who helped poor people. Friends and family give one another gifts and poems on this day.

Dutch children call Saint Nicholas Sinterklaas (SIN-ter-klahss). Over the years, many Dutch families moved to North America. In North America, Sinterklaas became known as Santa Claus.

The Dutch enjoy other events in spring and summer, too. The national holiday of the Netherlands is Koninginnedag (koh-nee-HEE-neh-dagh). This is the Queen's Official Birthday. The day honors the Dutch queen. It is celebrated every April 30. People do not have to work on this day. There are many parades and parties.

There are parades on Koninginnedag.

Hands On: Grow a Tulip

The tulip is the Netherlands' most famous flower. Many Dutch gardens are full of tulips. You can grow a tulip, too.

What You Need
A tulip bulb
Refrigerator
A pot that is 15 inches (38 centimeters) deep
Soil
Water

What You Do
1. Place the tulip bulb in your refrigerator or a cold place. Leave it there for two months. Make sure there is no fresh fruit by the bulb. Fruit kills the flower in bulbs.
2. Place five inches (13 centimeters) of soil in your pot.
3. Place the tulip bulb on the soil. Make sure the pointed end of the bulb is on top.
4. Cover the tulip bulb with eight inches (20 centimeters) of soil. Water your tulip bulb.
5. Place your pot in a cool place. After two weeks, move the pot to a sunny spot.
6. Water your tulip every week. Watch your tulip grow. Soon it will have a colorful bloom.

Learn to Speak Dutch

good-bye	Dag	(DAH)
good evening	Goede avond	(HOO-deh AH-vunt)
good morning	Goede morgen	(HOO-deh MOR-hen)
hello	Hallo	(HAH-loh)
I do not know.	Ik weet het niet.	(IK VEET UT NEET)
please	Alstublieft	(ALS-too-bleeft)
see you	Tot ziens	(TOT ZEENS)
thank you	Dank u	(DAHNK OO)

Words to Know

boar (BORE)—a wild pig

canal (kuh-NAL)—a specially built waterway

clog (KLOG)—a wooden shoe

dike (DEYK)—a strong wall built to keep water from flooding the land

fierljeppen (feerl-YEP-pen)—an old Dutch sport where people use a long pole to leap over things

gable (GAY-bul)—a part of a roof

uitsmijter (OUTS-may-ter)—a sandwich made with buttered bread and meat that is topped with fried eggs

Read More

Jacobsen, Karen. *The Netherlands*. Chicago: Children's Press, 1992.
Seward, Pat. *Netherlands*. New York: Marshall Cavendish, 1995.

Internet Sites

FactHound offers a safe, fun way to find Internet sites related to this book.

Go to *www.facthound.com*

He'll fetch the best sites for you!

Index